The Perfect Woman's Flaw
by
Patti R. Williams, Ph.D.

Bridge Publishing, Inc.
South Plainfield, NJ 07080

International Standard Book Number: 0-88270-701-9
Published by Bridge Publishing
South Plainfield, New Jersey 07080

Introduction

As a marriage counselor for the past twenty-five years, I have talked with many couples about their problems in interpersonal relationships. However, in the past few years, I have seen a specific pattern in the lives of the couples where the husband either wouldn't talk with his wife or showed interest in someone other than his wife. As I studied the behavior and personalities of these couples, I found one underlying similarity. Thus, the research and counseling sessions have prompted me to write *The Perfect Woman's Flaw*.

I want to make it clear that both men and women have flaws in their personalities, but this research will be addressing a common flaw of many women.

These pages have been written to identify the flaw and to suggest ways of overcoming this self-defeating behavior which alienates us in our relationships.

Other books by Patti Williams

Husbands! For Wives Only

Contents

1
The Perfect Woman: "In" Control?

Betty Sue sat at the kitchen table clutching her teacup until her knuckles were white. She wiped the tears from her eyes with her soiled apron. Her mind was racing; her thoughts were scrambled.

"How could Harry do this to me?" she wondered. "How could he have someone else?"

The hurt and pain were too sharp for her mind to linger there. Betty Sue tried to recall their eleven years together. She was a good wife. She kept herself up. She was attractive. She was educated, having finished college as one of the top students in her class. She held an executive position for seven years before little Josh came along.

She kept a neat home and lovely yard, and was a great decorator and organizer. She kept the family finances and handled the money well.

She had helped Harry, her husband, to organize and build his business. She gave dinner parties for his friends and business associates.

She was articulate and decisive within her family life. She was a good mother to little Josh, seeing to all his needs so that his father could spend more time with the business.

She was glad when Harry wanted to play golf with the guys. "Bless his heart," she thought, "he needs the time off."

She took care of Harry's mother's needs. His mom was eighty-three years old and needed someone to take her shopping, to the doctor's office, to the hairdresser, and to church on Sunday.

As Betty Sue reminisced about her good deeds, fine qualities, the fact that she was a good mom, and a perfect wife, she was stunned. "Then why doesn't Harry love me?" she asked herself. "Where is the flaw?"

A Spiritual Distortion

My research has shown that many women have a spiritual distortion known as *perfectionism*.

Webster's 7th New Collegiate Dictionary, '63 ed., defines *perfection* as "flawlessness" and "an exemplification of supreme excellence" and the word *perfectionism* as "a disposition to regard anything short of perfection as unacceptable.[1] Another way of phrasing it would be, "an exceedingly strong internal demand to perform constantly without flaw." [2]

Many forms of religious training, traditional western education and the media uphold perfectionist thinking. When one watches television, one sees ads for "perfect" soaps, food, vacations and other things. One also hears of the perfect romance, the perfect marriage, and the perfect family. The media seeks to convince us that they have all the "perfect" answers.

Perfectionists are amazing people. Most perfectionists that I have known are intelligent, articulate, achievers, organizers, creative competitors and are basically people-pleasers.

As a mother, wife or career person, the perfect woman could be considered a "superwoman." She can do it all. Take the mother role, for example. In this role, the perfect woman may direct the household, organize the children, and supervise the husband. She keeps on top of almost everything. She manages time well. She controls everyone and everything. As long as everyone is doing as she directs, the household runs smoothly and orderly.

As a career woman, the perfectionist often directs the staff, organizes the office and supervises the workload with grace and apparent ease.

This superwoman comes home from work and then cooks, cleans, does laundry, buys groceries - why, she can do it all!

Some women when they are young girls live in a family situation in which parents are demanding and give what we call "conditional love." These parents demand that their child live up to their expectation. They provide little affirmation but plenty of criticism. Young girls coming from this kind of background grow into adulthood trying to please their parents so that they will receive the attention that conditional love doesn't give. Adult women who come from such a background often develop a perfectionist personality. Becoming people-pleasers with a super ego, they have low self-esteem.

Webster's 7th New Collegiate Dictionary, '67 ed., has the definition of *esteem* as "high regard" and "to set a high value on".[3]

David Seamands writes: "When we speak of self-esteem, we mean that individuals place value on themselves as persons and consider themselves as having worth. Performance-grounded Christians do not feel good about themselves as persons, in spite of what they may have accomplished. However successful they may be in the eyes of others, they invariably belittle themselves - they literally tell themselves to "be little" so that they will not forget the small value they put on themselves, and their imagined insignificance in the sight of God and other people." [4]

Neil Warren writes, "Anger explosions proceed most often from the mouth. And that spray of verbal lead can be as deadly as a machine gun."[5] The explosions of anger he is referring to here are many faceted, their ultimate purpose is almost always the same: to punish the person, hit him between the eyes, to do him in. So whether the words are designed to place blame, to justify some action, or to let another person know that you won't take any more, they usually involve a high percentage of venomous put-downs. The attitude is, "I want to make her wrong, make her pay, or make her feel bad."

These verbal explosions are usually responses to unmet needs to feel complete or perfect. These bombshells are almost always directed at those people most significant in meeting our needs. As we find ourselves consistently exploding at the same person, we would do well to ask ourselves what needs we think that person is failing to meet for us. It is usually embarrassing, when after careful assessment we find that much of the time those needs are "fantasy needs" from our most irrational centers.

Perfectionists often unconsciously assume that their perceived needs should always get met. The whole world should revolve around them, nurture

5

them, and keep them satisfied. When others fail to meet this unrealistic expectation, the perfectionist feels wronged and blames others. She lets loose with carefully chosen "put-downers."

Warren points out the perfectionist's desire to say, "Pay very close attention to meeting my needs all the time. That's what should matter most to you."

Sometimes perfectionists have an unconscious need to be seen as perfect. Social approval becomes like a god for them. And they seem to operate on the assumption that such approval requires perfection. Since criticism indicates flaw, and flaw jeopardizes approval, perfectionists may explode in response to the slightest critical remark about them. Their psychic structure is fragile, based on their ability to secure other people's approval by being good enough.[6]

Along this line, some women seem to have difficulty in knowing who they are and who they ought to be. These same women have the identical performance standard for others as for themselves. They well up with anger, bitterness, and resentment when they don't measure up to their own performance standards and those of others. Often their anger turns into depression.

Women who have this perfectionist personality feel that they must do things right. They usually work alone because they think no one else can do a job as well as they can. They feel they are always right, and surprisingly a large percentage of the time they really are.

In order for the perfect woman to feel in control, she must play a game with herself. Marian Adderholdt-Elliot, in her book *Perfectionism: What's Bad About Being Too Good*, lists eight games perfectionists play:

•Mood Swinging

To set a goal and accomplish it makes one feel great. But to set another goal and not accomplish it makes one feel awful. Perfectionists experience mood swings such as this often. It's exhausting.

•Playing the Numbers Game

The quantity of achievements or actions becomes more important than the quality. No number is ever high enough; perfectionists just keep counting.

•Telescopic Thinking

Perfectionists use both ends of a telescope when viewing their achievements. When looking at the goals they haven't met, they use the magnifying end so the goals appear much larger than they really are. But when looking at goals they have met, perfectionists use the "minifying" end: these goals appear minute and insignificant.

•Focusing on the Future

Perfectionists don't savor success: even as each goal is accomplished, they're already planning their future.

•Pining Over the Past

"If only" thoughts tend to keep perfectionists stuck in the same old groove of the same old record.

•Putting Goals First

Goals come first over fun, friends, or one's own good health.

•Getting it Right

Perfectionists are dissatisfied with anything but perfection.

•"All-or-Nothing" Thinking

Perfectionists are not satisfied unless they have it all. [7]

As the eight games listed above demonstrate, the minds of perfectionists use a number of tricks to protect the picture they have of themselves.

In 1984, when a group of women students from the University of Georgia were tested to determine the relationship between perfectionism and self-concept, a fascinating pattern emerged: the higher the perfectionism score, the lower the self-concept score. The young women were tying their identities to their performance.

When a woman ties her identity to her performance she is making a poor choice. In setting unrealistic goals and pushing herself to achieve more and faster, the woman muddles her mind and body. She creates her own stress. She is afraid to take risks and fearful of not getting the approval she has been raised to appreciate.

Marian Adderholdt-Elliot writes about the shy writer who completed a lengthy manuscript but was afraid to submit it to a publisher. What if no one accepted it? She wasn't sure she could take rejection. Today there are twenty-five million copies of her book in print, around the world and in several languages. Her name was Margaret Mitchell and the title of her book is *Gone With the Wind*.

The perfect woman often loses her joy when she should be experiencing one of the happiest moments of her life; for example, the wedding day of her son. Helen came into my office for a counseling session. She was noticeably upset. As Helen's story unfolded, she began wringing her hands and lowering her head.

Helen began discussing her only son's engagement. She was thrilled with the young lady he had chosen and looked forward to the wedding day. However, as the wedding plans began to take shape, Helen had her own agenda. But as the mother of the groom her input didn't seem to be appreciated.

As the time drew nearer for the wedding, Helen became involved in planning her rehearsal dinner, making her invitation list, and looking for her wedding dress. The night of the rehearsal dinner finally came; however, many things went wrong: the restaurant did not have the tables set up as expected; her own family didn't get there on time; and her husband came in a little tipsy. On top of that, her son spent more time with the bride's family than with his own. The service was inadequate, the food wasn't very good, and she just wasn't appreciated for planning such a fine rehearsal dinner.

To make matters worse, the next day she and her husband had a disagreement before they arrived at the church. She felt snubbed by the bride's parents. The priest totally ignored her. So what should have been a joyful time was a very unhappy day for her.

What was the problem? As we talked, she realized that things had not been done to her expectations. Therefore, what should have been a joy was an unpleasant experience. We discussed the old adage, "When you are the mother of the groom all you have to do is wear a beige dress and keep your mouth shut."

False or too high expectations for self and others is one characteristic of the perfectionist person. There seems to be a thin line between realistic "desires" for some situation to turn out right, and idealistic "expectations" for it to be perfect. When a perfectionist expects to control every detail of any given circumstance so that it will turn out her way, then she is setting herself up for hurt, disappointment, anger, frustration, and failure. On the other hand if one desires an event to be as nice as can be, and is flexible accepting the fact that things don't always go according to plans - then one's attitude will help turn even a disaster into a tolerable, pleasant, or joyous experience.

Randy and Nanci Alcorn, authors of *Women Under Stress*, have some interesting thoughts on this subject. They maintain that perceptions - much more than circumstances - are the building blocks with which we construct our life. There is a sense in which we literally create the world we live in. If it is empty, irritating, boring, hectic, or hurried, it is because we have perceived it that way and thereby made it that way. No matter what the circumstances, our view of life determines our level of joy and contentment.

We are not discussing "positive thinking" here as much as biblical thinking. Some ungodly people are "positive thinkers," but they have no time for the doctrine of sin and the reality of true

11

moral guilt and human accountability to God. Neither are we discussing the philosophy behind many of the success books, and the innumerable seminars spun off from them, which define success in terms of the accumulation of wealth.

Our thinking here is rooted in biblical facts, based on the resurrection of Christ, which causes the believer's optimism to be based squarely on realism. God is real; the incarnation and atonement are real; the second coming is real. We think in this positive perspective because the truth is inescapably positive. Thus, having a biblical perspective is seeing life as God sees it. It is the ability to get past immediate circumstances to see God's ultimate plan. [8]

An illustration of *perspective* is what Joshua and Caleb demonstrated; it's what the other ten spies lacked (Num. 13-14). Joshua and Caleb entered the Promised Land and saw land, fruit, the potential for prosperity, and a place for their families to live and worship God.

On the other hand, the ten spies went to the same land and saw something entirely different. They saw a land of *giants* - great men of battle, who made conquering the land seem impossible. They saw the giants as even bigger than God.

Not so with Josh and Caleb. They saw the same giants, but somehow were not intimidated.

They envisioned God in His majesty on the throne, and could look at the same set of circumstances and see a completely different picture than the others saw - a picture both optimistic and realistic.

The perfectionist needs to observe Proverbs 19:21, "Many are the plans in a man's or woman's heart, but it is the Lord's purpose that prevails." If we want to be truly fulfilled in this life, it will come about by our unclenching our fists from our own plans and giving ourselves over to His purpose, whether visible or not. Stress and strain cannot stand in the face of the right perspective such as Proverbs 18:14, "A man's or woman's spirit sustains him in sickness, but a crushed spirit who can bear?" As our perspective goes, so go our weddings, vacations, jobs, dishes, our car pool, our whole life.

The Alcorns point us to the popular children's story, *Alexander and the Terrible, Horrible, No Good, Very Bad Day,* to illustrate that what happens to Alexander are the usual kinds of irritations that happen to us all each day. These annoying experiences are simply part of being alive in this far-from-perfect world. Our loss of perspective magnifies all these little irritations. It's worth thinking about for just a moment. If today was a bad day for you, ask yourself, "When was the last time I had a normal day?" It wasn't Alexander's circumstances that made it a terrible, horrible, no good, very bad day. It was simply his perspective and his response to circumstances.

Too many of us rejoice when our circumstances are good, and get depressed when our circumstances are bad. But as Christians we are to "rejoice in the Lord always" (Phil. 4:4-6). The perfectionist finds this almost impossible to do!

By this time you may be asking, "Is the perfect woman really in control?"

Patricia Gundry, in her book *The Complete Woman,* writes that you need to be able to tell the difference between perfectionism and balanced living.

Perfectionism says, "I have to do this!" Balanced living says, "I will try to do it." When it doesn't work, the perfectionist says, "It's no good," or "I'm no good," or "It will never work," or "I can't." The individual with balanced living says, "It didn't work this time," or "It didn't work yet," or "Maybe I had better change my tactics," or "I will reassess the situation."

Balanced living is relaxed; perfectionistic living is uptight. Balanced living is flexible; perfectionism is win-or-lose. People who aim for a balanced life are miserable a small amount of the time. Perfectionists are miserable much of the time. The main trouble with perfectionism is that it is impossible to live up to, thus it is unrealistic.[9]

It isn't difficult to see many problems arising in our lives as women, mates, mothers, and workers when we live in the perfectionist mode.

David Seamands has gotten thousands of letters and phone calls from readers of his book, *Healing for Damaged Emotions*. The correspondence and calls reinforce his conviction that "neurotic perfectionism" is one of the most common emotional problems affecting Christians today.

Seamands warns us to make sure we do not confuse the biblical doctrine of Christian perfection with its greatest hindrance and counterfeit, neurotic perfectionism. Biblical perfection is reaching a level of maturity in which the holiness of Christ is imparted to us by the infilling Holy Spirit, so that we are enabled to live a life of habitual victory over sin. Like justification, this sanctification is purely a gift of God. We received it by grace and live it by faith.

It does not depend upon perfectly performing works, but on faith in God's perfect performance. Scripture admonishes us to aim for this level of sanctified living.

Christian perfection goes by many names, depending on one's theological background. Unfortunately, it is called by some the "Higher Life," or the "Deeper Life," or the "Spirit-Filled Life," but that is because these Christians seem content to live on a lower, more shallow, and half-filled level of life. [10] The normal Christian life is the healthy pursuit of excellence by those who, out of gratitude for God's love and grace, want to please Him and be their best, especially on His terms.

Neurotic perfectionists counterfeit true Christian perfection. They strain compulsively and constantly to make themselves acceptable to God and to measure their relationship to Him in terms of performance and accomplishment. As Seamands so beautifully puts it, "They are restive achievers, not resting believers." He indicates that the root cause of this is an unbiblical concept of God, that views the God of the Universe as unpleasable.

The God of this erroneous view is an increasingly demanding tyrant who requires perfect performance. He is a punitive judge who has no tolerance for imperfection. At the slightest failure, He expresses His displeasure and covers imperfect Christians with condemnation and guilt. This leads perfectionistic Christian women to twist the truth, so that they rate their behavior before God higher than their relationship to God. They tend to place conduct before faith, work before worship, and performance higher than relationship. [11]

Seamands goes on to say that perfectionists have oversensitive consciences and live under "the tyranny of the oughts." So a perfectionist is a person who tries to placate her anxiety by false humility. Belittling herself, she overemphasizes doctrines, duties, rules and regulations.

These people are given to mood swings and often to depression because, even though they constantly try harder, they are guilt-ridden and fearful. When we base our relationship to God on performance and not on grace, then a sense of failure and guilt follows. This robs us of our joy and may even drive some to emotional or spiritual breakdown.

Christians often suffer from degrees of perfectionism. Even people who have come from the best of homes, and ideal situations, battle with wrong concepts of God.

One of the most amazing things about the love of God, writes Seamands, is that God "accepts us in spite of our distorted pictures of Him, and works with us until we gradually come to know Him as He truly is."[12]   Many of us begin our pilgrimage in the Christian life with a mixture of law and grace. Only by experiencing God's great faithfulness in and through our many failures do we eventually come to a place where we can really understand that line in the hymn, "Rock of Ages" - "Nothing in my hands I bring, simply to Thy cross I cling."

In spite of earnest, faithful disciplines, some find it difficult to grow out of the pattern of perfectionism into the wonderful freedom found by maturing in Christ. When this happens, they unknowingly create a legalistic, graceless home atmosphere of conditional love, which carries over into the next generation.

By the grace of God it does not have to be this way. The Holy Spirit can bring such Christians to an awareness of the disease of perfectionism and to a cure. Reading books like this one can lead to understanding and to progress. Hopefully, these perfectionists can experience God's grace in the very depths of their souls.

What are the trade-offs for the perfect woman? If she's too independent, she's not a team player. If she's always right, she alienates herself from others. If she must always win, no one will want to play with her.

How does a woman get herself into this situation? In the next chapter, we will explore how women get themselves into this perfectionist mode.

1. *Webster's Seventh New Collegiate Dictionary,* G. & C. Merriam Company, Editors (Springfield: G. & C. Merriam Co., 1963), p. 626.

2. J. Croghan, "The Psychology of Art." *American Artist Magazine,* June 1987, p. 14.

3. *Webster's Seventh New Collegiate Dictionary,* G. & C. Merriam Company, Editors (Springfield: G. & E. Merriam Co., 1967), p. 284.

4. David Seamands, *Healing Grace* (Wheaton: Victor Books, 1988), p. 17.

5. Neil Clark Warren, *Make Anger Your Ally* (Garden City: Doubleday & Company, Inc., 1983), p. 40.

6. Ibid., p. 41.

7. Marian Adderholdt-Elliot, *Perfectionism* (Minneapolis: Free Spirit Publishing, Inc., 1987), pp. 18-20.

8. Randy and Nanci Alcorn, *Women Under Stress* (Portland: Multnomah Press, 1986) p. 52.

9. Patricia Gundry, *The Complete Woman* (Garden City: Doubleday & Co., Inc., 1981), p. 231.

10. David A. Seamands, *Healing of Memories* (Wheaton: Victor Books, 1988), p. 117.

11. Ibid., p. 119.

12. Ibid.

2
The Perfect Woman:
"Put" in Control

How did the perfect woman get in control?
Erik Erikson, the psychologist, teaches that children between the ages of six and twelve are at a
risk for becoming perfectionists if they are re-
warded for things they do rather than for the
personal qualities they have and are developing.
In other words, the child who is praised for bring-
ing home perfect papers but not for being a nice
person, having a sense of humor, being playful,
taking risks, showing kindness and gentleness,
and being a good friend is likely to think that work
is the most important part of life or that it will
bring rewards.[1] Little girls want attention. One

way to get it is to be "good" (or should we say "perfect"?). Because of the praise this brings, a little girl may develop into adulthood becoming all things to all people. She becomes a "caretaker." She tries to please. She becomes very helpful.

Women who are perfectionist tie their identities to their performance. As long as they are performing they tend to feel good about themselves; however, when they can't perform or be center stage they develop a low self-esteem.

The Myth of Perfection

A popular myth says, "A well-adjusted, successful person has no faults." Myths like this teach children that, in order to gain acceptance, it is necessary to pretend to "have it all together" even when they don't. Given the naive belief some have that everyone else is perfect, and the knowledge that oneself isn't, it is easy to see how one's self-concept can suffer.

In developing a self-concept, newborn babies learn to judge themselves only through the way others treat them. The amount of time a parent lets a newborn baby cry before attending to its needs gives the child a measure of how important he or she is to the parent. Every day, a child is bombarded with scores of messages.

Some of these messages are: "You're so cute," "I love you," "What a big girl (or boy)." Other messages are: "Can't you do anything right?", "What's the matter with you?", "You're so bad," or "Leave me alone, you're driving me crazy!"

These comments (evaluations) that significant others make to us *are the mirrors by which we know ourselves.*

Biblical Background

The Book of Genesis records the story of humanity's wrong choice and the terrible consequences which followed. It is known in theological circles as the Fall.

Human beings, created to live forever, over and above all other creatures, yet under God, got off to a bad start because Adam and Eve, the first humans, listened to Satan. Satan's fall is recorded in Isaiah 14:12-15 and Luke 10:18. His problem was simple: he desired to be God, and he refused to accept who he was. As a result, God had to deal with his rebellion. God cast Satan to the bottom of the universe, which became his domain.

This fallen angel sowed the deadly seeds of temptation in Eve's mind until she began to question the goodness of God's *perfect character*. Blinded by Satan's accusations concerning the truthfulness of God's Holy Word, Adam and Eve

23

did not see God's loving limitation not to eat from the tree of the knowledge of good and evil as God's gracious provision to enable His children to enjoy all the other provisions in the garden even more fully. Adam and Eve fell for Satan's misinformation concerning God's limitation. Satan convinced them it was the cruel prohibition of a hateful oppressor. They chose not to accept God's word in the matter, and decided to do things their way. Their only alternatives, at this point, were to do things God's way or their own way. They could trust and obey God or distrust Him and decide for themselves. They could either continue to live in a trusting relationship with their heavenly Father and thus enjoy all His perfect gifts, or they could refuse to remain in that beautiful situation and take matters into their own *control*.

Unfortunately, for them and for all humanity down through the ages, Adam and Eve chose to rebel against God and His control over their lives. They decided to take things into their own hands, refusing to accept their limitations. Even though they had perfection - being a little less than God himself - they wanted more. St. Augustine put it this way:

"And what is the origin of our evil will but pride? For 'pride is the beginning of sin' (Ecclesiastes 10:13). And what is pride but the craving for undue exaltation? And this is undue exaltation, when the soul abandons him to whom it ought to cleave as its end, and becomes a kind of end in itself."[2]

In trying to become *like* God, Adam and Eve failed. They actually became *less* than they were intended to be. They could not achieve the glory and perfection that belongs only to God. Instead, they lost the only kind of perfection they had, which was a gift from God to be in His likeness. The upshot of all this was the introduction of imperfection.

The original, innate human perfections are now gone. We can never retrieve them through our own efforts, no matter how hard we work at it. This frustrates the performance-oriented Christian woman. She begins to say, "*If only* I could do well enough, *if only* someone else would work harder, *if only* people could understand, *if only* God would do something about it. After all, it *ought* to be, so it *could* be. It *would* be, *if only*...."

Humans lost many things in the Fall besides the performance fantasy many women try to live by. We lost *natural* perfection. In Romans 8: 19-22 Paul describes how the whole creation is now imperfect, groaning, awaiting the day when it "will be liberated from its bondage and decay." As Seamands puts it, "*Chaos* has now entered into the *cosmos*."[3]

What else have we lost? We have lost *physical* perfection. Almost everywhere we look there are injury and suffering, disease and deformities, deterioration and death. Not only that, but we have lost *mental* perfection. Think of the computer-like brain Adam must have had to classify and name "each and every living creature," which implies a process of the brain we no longer possess. Of course, a few, autistic people hint of this capability. So do a few Michelangelos, Einsteins, and Newtons. These people we call geniuses, which simply means we acknowledge that what they have received is a gift, not something they have achieved.

Along this line of thinking, Seamands describes his wonder at the incredible assumptions some performance-minded and perfectionistic Christians live with. He said that he listened to Angela tell him all the things for which she felt guilty. Her list got longer and longer, and she became very emotional as she heaped failure after failure on herself. Lines of strain showed on her face. It was obvious that she was, as she put it, "living on the nub."

The more Seamands talked with her the more he realized that the melancholy spell she found herself in had to be broken. He leaned forward and said eagerly, "Angela, may I touch you?"

This startled her and she backed away from him. She said, "What?"

Again he asked her, "May I touch you? You see, it's been a long time since I've seen such a divine being."

She responded, "What do you mean?"

"What I mean, Angela, is that only some kind of god-like creature could expect to do all the things you listed, let alone to do them perfectly. You have absolutely divine expectations. Where did you ever get the notion that you or anyone else were expected to do all those things? What I hear you saying is that you feel guilty because you can't do *everything and do it flawlessly.*"

Angela sat silent for quite a while. Then she hung her head and cried quietly.

Then what she said was amazing. "Do you know what I'm thinking?" she asked. "It's crazy and I'm ashamed to tell you. But this confirms what has been dawning on me lately. Somewhere, a long time ago, I began to take seriously what my folks used to call me - 'Angel.' I can't believe it. I felt they expected so much of me that I began to play the part of an angel. I can't put all the blame on them - I brought a lot of this on myself, trying to feel special."

For this young lady, it was a Spirit-revealed moment of self-awareness which started her on a new pilgrimage of grace and freedom from the performance trap.[4]

27

Not only have we lost natural, physical, and mental perfection, but according to Seamands, we have lost *emotional* perfection as well. All we have to do is a little honest reflection to see an array of our negative emotions - fear, worry, anger, rage, jealousy, and self-despising.

In addition to this we have lost *relational* perfection. This is where that *emotional* being out of balance affects us most. That beautiful transparency which must have existed in the Garden between Adam and Eve is now gone (Gen. 2:24-25). Often we are *ashamed* of our sexuality, even within marriage. Meaningful friendship, companionship, Christian fellowship, or the deeper intimacies of sexual oneness within marriage do not come about easily and naturally. They require a lot of effort. This matter of relationships will be dealt with more fully in chapter three.

But of all the things we have lost in this Fall, perhaps the most important is *spiritual* perfection. This is the fundamental loss from which all others come. Our *God-centeredness* has become *self-centeredness*. The human personality, once in *perfect harmony* with God, nature, others, and self, is now *in conflict* with everything.

Seamands says that what was "intended to be called 'son' has been defaced. The center has been displaced with an 'I' so it spells 'sin.' What was perfect is fallen, bent, and broken."[5] He adds that we have lost not only the perfect, but also our ability to earn, perform, or retrieve the perfect. We truly live in Paradise lost and there is no way back.

This forces us to realize that the major sin problem of perfectionism is rooted in the theological aspect of our lives. If the ultimate cure for our predicament is the grace of God, then the ultimate cause of the behavior is our failure to understand, experience, and live out grace at every level of our lives. This leads us to believe that any attempt to achieve right relationships by any means other than God's total plan of grace will indeed be futile. Having said that, we can go on now to see some additional reasons why women are put into this performance-oriented mode.

Background

From the time we were little girls, many of us have tended to build some lies into our essence. One destructive lie is "If I don't do right, I won't be loved." Another lie is, "If I can't be like mommy and daddy want me to be, I won't belong." Consequently, the little girl who believes these lies has constant anxiety and fear and is always striving.

Childish minds connect performing with love. We might think, "If I don't do it right, mommy won't love me." We come to believe that not performing earns rejection. Then, when someone shows us love, we think we do not deserve it. Either we won't receive the love offered, or else we are assailed by false guilt.

Children will act bad, and will need to be disciplined by firm hands, and given parameters, while being warmly held and accepted even when they are at their worst. A child who feels unconditional love feels secure.

John and Paula Sandford write in *The Transformation of the Inner Man,* "Uptight, rigid demands for behavior, without affection, clamp upon children the manacles of control, 'You will not be loved unless you can deserve it.' Once that lie is grafted in, it becomes the governing trunk to all our fruit, all our actions flow through that stem."[6]

Children need an atmosphere where they feel their needs are met because of who they are, not because of what they do. David Seamands gives the following formula: "Rules and Regulations minus Relationships equals Resentment and Rebellion." Rules and regulations must be put in the context of loving relationships that are full of grace or they will result in frustration and resentment.

A friend told this story about when she was a little girl. She was in a baton-twirling contest. As she performed perfectly to the music, strutting off the stage, her teacher leaned over and told her how perfectly she had done her routine. With a face aglow and feeling of excitement in her heart she went directly to her parents. Her mother said, "It was a good performance, but your panties were showing beneath your tights."

A feeling of self-worth is devastated when a little girl hears this kind of comment. She may consciously decide to become another person. This happens deep in her personality even below the level of self-awareness. She may think, "I am not accepted or loved as I am. Nothing I can do pleases them. So I'll become something else. Then maybe I'll be acceptable and loveable!"

Slowly but surely an idealized fantasy self emerges, a super-self which will try to live up to all the expectations and demands of the parents. The child begins to feel special and may develop an "I'm better than others" attitude. When this super-self grows up it becomes an "I'm entitled to" attitude. This creation of false self is often the price of emotional survival.

Doctors Meyer Friedman and Ray H. Rosenman use the term "type A behavior," which describes a driven personality type. Studies have shown that type A people tend to be angry or hostile more than others. They keep their feelings locked in for a long time until they boil over. They also hold grudges for a long time.

Type A's have a lot of good qualities, like a high energy level and the ability to get things done. Many are leaders and hard workers. Many are perfectionists.

In fact, type A's and perfectionists have a lot in common. Here are some of the similarities researchers have uncovered:

•A higher percentage of firstborn children are perfectionists and a higher percentage of firstborn children are type A's.

•Both may have parents who are overly critical and controlling. Parents of type A's are often reluctant to let them try things on their own. Parents of perfectionists find it difficult to give them the freedom to experience trial-and-error learning.

•Just as perfectionist children often have perfectionist parents, type A children often have type A parents. And maybe those children grow up to be perfectionists and type A's themselves - and raise still more perfectionists and type A's.

•Both tend to take on more and more activities and to squeeze them into shorter and shorter time periods. Both think they can beat the clock.

•Both are prone to stress-related illnesses from overloading their circuits and not getting enough rest.

Are you a type A person? Find out by reading the following statements. Respond to each with "I'm like that sometimes" or "I'm never like that."

1. I feel hostile or angry much of the time.
2. I tend to talk, walk, and/or eat rapidly.
3. I'm extremely competitive.
4. I find myself scheduling more work into shorter time periods and leaving less time for play.
5. I often try to do two things at once.
6. It's very hard for me to relax.
7. I'm impatient - I hate standing in lines.
8. I take pride in being able to do things faster and faster.
9. I seldom notice or take pleasure in beauty or nature.
10. I hardly ever listen to other people's opinions.

If you answered "I'm like that sometimes" on most of the above questions then there is a strong likelihood that you were a little girl who wanted attention. When you became a grown woman you tended to perform for attention and self-esteem. The "type A" designation of a woman can be characterized by most or all of the following:

- Achievement orientation
- Free-floating anxiety
- Time urgency
- Trying to do several things at once
- Excessively high expectations of self and others
- Uneasiness
- Impatience
- Intolerance
- Aggressiveness
- Competitiveness
- Frustration
- Anger
- Strained relationship (we'll look at this in the next chapter)
- Driven personality - guilt feelings when relaxing[7]

This type A woman is a stress-prone personality with a much greater chance of having a heart attack, stroke, or other very serious ailment. She is also preoccupied with time. Almost everything she does is done quickly, with regular glances at the clock. She hates to wait in lines or take time to go to the doctor.

34

"The type A treats life as a 100 meter run - and dies at 150 meters," write Randy and Nanci Alcorn.[8]

Jane Brody, in an article in *Reader's Digest*, writes that studies seem to indicate that women who work outside the home are more often type A's than are homemakers, although plenty of homemakers are also type A's. Brody writes, "These women are more likely than the type B's to have unhappy marriages."[9] (We will look at this more closely in the next chapter.)

So how does a woman get "put" in control? Because of her desire to please and to perform, she tends to become a perfectionist. She takes control! She tends to intimidate those around her. She is self-assured. She is demanding and domineering.

This perfectionist wife, mother, and/or worker, is prone to think she can change the people with whom she gets involved. These perfectionists believe that others can't help but improve while in their company - and they're very willing to push the process along. "Let me make a suggestion," when spoken by a perfectionist, turns into "Do it my way."

The *helpful personality* is another characteristic of a perfectionist. The woman who has a perfectionist personality likes to give advice or opinions on things or to people. She is almost always trying to be helpful. At a meeting she is the one who holds up her hand and volunteers for whatever. She wants the job done and knows she can do it better than anyone else. It doesn't matter how much responsibility she has already accepted - taking on one more thing won't be too much. Besides, she thinks she will be appreciated for her good work, which will make her feel better about herself.

The helpful personality who wants to control, and as a result seems to always feel the need to give advice, is illustrated in the following story.

A lady came into my office for counseling with a heavy heart concerning her thirty-year-old son. She was distraught over the fact that her son just did not seem to grow up and take responsibility. He continued to flounder in his vocation, changing from one job to another, and moved into and out of her house often. She had become tired of giving him money and supporting him, but she kept saying to herself, "He needs me."

As the lady told her story, she revealed that she had taken control of her son and told him what to do and how to do it over the years. He did not know how to make a decision on his own, and when he did, in her opinion, it was always a poor one.

What precipitated the problem this time, she thought, was that he had moved out of her house on the weekend and moved in with a girlfriend.

Now, three days later, he was asking to move back into her house. It was driving her crazy because she saw it as his problem but could not recognize that it was also because of her "helpful" way over the years that helped mold her thirty-year-old son into what he was.

Once she became aware of her own contribution to her son's problem, she could begin to change herself and hopefully get both out of the horrible cycle they were in.

You can see this helpful personality very often and easily in the workplace. Inevitably, it seems that at least one person wants to run the office in a business or organization - and it is not the one designated to do so. A friend told me about an incident in her office. She said that they were interviewing a woman for a position. The woman was making suggestions, one right after the other, about how they could better run their business. Even though she did not know much, she was handing out her suggestions. Not surprisingly, they did not hire the woman for the job. Even though the lady had excellent qualifications, she talked herself out of a job by being too free with her advice and by being too helpful.

A perfectionist, even in her helpful way, can often come across as being critical. This was evident on one occasion when a friend shared a story about a visit her best friend made to her married daughter's house.

As they entered her daughter's home this woman said, "You usually keep this place cleaner - it's not usually this messed up."

As these two ladies toured the daughter's house, they went into the little girl's room. It looked like a typical three-year-old's room.

The grandmother insisted on showing her friend some dresses she had made for her granddaughter. As the lady's daughter opened the closet and began showing the beautiful little dresses, the mother commented, "Why, some of these aren't even ironed. Why haven't you ironed them?"

Then the mother started saying things like, "These pictures on the wall are placed in the wrong portion of the walls. Your hair doesn't look as nice as it could; what have you done to it?" A constant barrage of criticisms came under the guise of "helpful hints." Now we have a good idea why the daughter and mother have such a strained relationship and why the daughter has low self-esteem.

In many situations, helpful advice is not really warranted. This often happens in a second-marriage situation. The man's children from a former marriage are having problems and he feels depressed. As a father, he feels he has neglected his family in the past and wasn't the father he could have been.

Now his second wife, who is the perfectionist personality, can quickly diagnose the case and give him a perfect solution and tell him exactly what he should have done and what he can do now. She simply jumps right in and gives unwanted, unsolicited advice.

The perfectionist woman comes across to almost everyone as a person so "in control." These ladies can "take charge" and "oversee" everything in their path, and usually do a good job. This behavior often gets her into hot water and into situations where she gets hurt.

The dynamics of a hurting perfectionist are interesting to watch. Because they are so busy giving advice and help, they give the appearance of being on top of things. But they have their bad moments, and when they do, they usually crumble. This occurs because other people are unaware of the person's sensitivity and what is going on inside of them - they seem so "together." However, they are usually screaming inside, yet no one knows it.

They crave attention and support, but do not know how to get it because very few people believe they are hurting. It is hard to tell, sometimes, if these people even have a heart.

Again, we ask, how does a woman get "put" in control? As we have seen, a perfectionist personality has been forming from early childhood. This *spiritual distortion* continues into adulthood unless the woman becomes aware of her personality.

Take the case of Moraine. She grew up in a small family with a father, mother, and younger brother. Moraine's father was a career man in the United States Army. He ran his family just like he ran his platoon. He was in charge! He was always right! He wanted everything perfect for his wife and family. He was a gruff and domineering person.

Moraine and her family moved often and she had to learn to make new friends constantly. Adjusting to new situations was a way of life.

She did not receive much attention from her father. Her mother was always doting over her younger brother. Therefore, Moraine became withdrawn into her own little fantasy land. She felt in her heart that her father and mother did not love her and did not give her the attention she wanted so badly. She kept thinking that if she made good grades, it would please her parents. So she worked doubly hard at making good grades. But her parents never seemed to praise her enough.

She thought that, if she did everything to please her parents and little brother, they would love her more. But poor Moraine never felt loved.

As she grew into her teen years she was terribly attracted to the opposite sex. She thought that boys noticed her and believed they thought she was cute and smart. She loved the attention she received from her boyfriends.

However, this attention made her mother and father feel more and more uncomfortable, so they continued to criticize her more and more. This made Moraine feel less loved.

As she grew into young adulthood and finished college, Moraine met Jeff, fell head over heels in love and married him.

Things went well at first, but in her eagerness to please and to be perfect, Moraine began to run her household like her father had run his platoon. She took over all duties and responsibilities because she felt Jeff was not quite as good as she was at doing things around the house, paying the bills, working in the yard or running the business. She began to suggest, criticize, analyze and scold when Jeff was around her.

Their communication was nil, because Jeff would not talk with her due to her domineering personality. Thus, after a few years, Jeff started seeing the secretary at work. He finally asked Moraine for a divorce.

This illustration is just one of many that come into a counselor's office. How does a woman get "put" in control? She *takes* control!

1.   Marion Adderholdt-Elliott, *Perfectionism* (Minneapolis: Free Spirit Publishing, Inc.,1987), p. 11.

2.   David Seamands, *Healing Grace* (Wheaton: Victor Books, 1988), p. 61.

3.   Ibid., p. 62.

4.   Ibid., pp. 64-65.

5.   Ibid.

6.   John and Paula Sandford, *The Transformation of the Inner Man* (Tulsa: Victory House, Inc., 1987), p. 11.

7.   Randy and Nanci Alcorn, *Women Under Stress*, (Portland: Multnomah Press, 1986), p. 42.

8.   Ibid., p. 43.

9.   Jane Brody, "Become a 'Type B'," *Reader's Digest*, (April 1981), pp. 87-89.

3
The Perfect Woman: "Out" of Control

The perfectionist works hard, but for the wrong reasons. She requires constant affirmation (unconsciously demanding it, sometimes verbally). She cannot handle criticism well. Her security is not found in God and herself, but in what people think of her. She is dependent on the reactions of others. Reproofs are taken defensively, not as signs of acceptance and love, but as rejection.

Perfectionists give affection only in terms of how well the people around them have behaved. These people are afraid to try new things. Fear of failure rises more out of what loved ones and others will think of them than how failure may hurt another. The need to be in control reaches the point of idolatry.

Such women have little center of their own, and must act whatever the group model is. This explains why so many women are double-minded - feeling one way and acting another. Temptations pull together two powerful drives: one, to break out of the mold; and two, to belong to the group which presents the temptation.

These women have no identity. They begin to feel angry and frustrated, living like two different people. They are often angry and vindictive.

Take the example of Jan. Jan worked in a bank. She was a perfectionist - a very detailed person. As she worked with her co-workers, she was always angry. She had a hard time coming under authority with her boss.

Yet, you would never know how unhappy she was. She would laugh and smile with others.

Then one day it happened. Jan had had enough. She exploded! Everyone around her was shocked. She attacked her boss and anyone in her path. She was demanding. She showed bitterness and re-sentment. Jan had displayed her bright side for just so long and now was showing her dark side.

Her selfish, controlling self raised its ugly head above all her relationships. Everyone was aston-ished. The boss reprimanded her and said that if it happened again he would let her go.

Poor Jan. She never understood that *she* was the problem. Her own selfish, controlling desires took over. Her relationship with her co-workers could never be trusted again and her boss lost all respect for her.

The woman who is a perfectionist usually overpowers the man in a marriage relationship. She comes across as domineering, exacting and demanding. Because these wives are so good at their tasks they initiate a lot of power over their husbands.

Such a wife takes away her husband's self-esteem. This type of woman is always right - at least she thinks she is. Her ideas, plans and suggestions are so much better than her husband's. She's always telling him what to do or how to do it. She criticizes what he does. Because of this overbearing behavior, the man often rebels or gets frustrated and becomes a wimp.

The wife in a perfectionist relationship takes control of every aspect of the marriage and leaves no responsibility for her husband. This not only takes away his self-esteem, but his responsibility as well. In his frustration he may well rebel and give all leadership up to "Mrs. Perfect," then he may start looking for someone who is "imperfect."

To be sure, this does not give a husband the right to go looking for another woman. It is true that he allows his wife to take over. But he doesn't know how to handle the situation. This is often the case.

Take the case of Andrew and Gloria. This young, married couple have been married for three years. Andrew loves Gloria. He is a hard worker. He holds down a good job. He makes a decent living and gives Gloria most things a young bride would desire.

But Gloria is miserable. Andrew works too hard and too long. He doesn't talk to her. He doesn't dress right. He has quirky, little, irritating habits. On and on there are things wrong with Andy.

Gloria doesn't realize that early in the marriage she would critique Andy for every little thing he did. They would have guests over for supper and, while Andy was grilling the meat, Gloria would keep grilling him on how to do it. When the meat was done, she would tell him how to carve it. She complained in front of guests that his elbows were on the table, about the way he chewed his food, the way he held his fork, and on and on. When Andrew tried to share something exciting with Gloria, she would ask questions, grill him and then criticize him. Her favorite expression, often said in a shrill voice, was "What do you want to do that for?"

Andy finally became quiet. Gloria not only put him down, she overreacted before hearing the whole story. He finally rebelled and decided to say nothing.

This is a typical scenario of how relationships begin to break down.

The perfect woman has high expectations of how things "should" be. When these expectations are not met, she becomes hurt. Relationships become broken.

The perfectionist continues to play the tape in her mind over and over: "If I don't do it, no one else will." No matter how much she complains about the pressures of life, she will not let go, because having those pressures assures her that she is wanted and needed. Only perfectionism assures her that she is valued.

The perfectionist is *compulsive*. There are only twenty-four hours in a day, and yet, she tries to squeeze in more. Because of her compulsive behavior, she is often impatient and almost always running behind time. No matter how overextended she may be, she continues to complain. This gives her a sense of urgency and drama. Having a tight schedule makes her feel important.

Because of her perpetually being busy, she has little time for feeling. The perpetual motion creates a convincing illusion of purpose. But in truth she barely has time to get to where she is going, much less know if it's the right place to be.

Perfectionists leave little room for error. They tend to be note takers. They tend to be in a constant state of anxiety. They often feel on the edge of a nervous breakdown.

No matter how much the perfectionist accomplishes, she is always on the down side. Her identity is based on multiple roles (friend, mother, employee, and wife). Because of her effort to be perfect and to prove herself in each area, she winds up feeling haunted by her incompleteness rather than gladdened by her successes.

The perfect woman perpetuates an image of self-sufficiency, rarely asking for help and refusing it when it is offered. A good illustration of this is the wife who does everything for everyone and goes around huffing and puffing because no one will pick up after themselves. She might be the perfect wife who invites the in-laws for supper or a holiday dinner and insists on doing everything herself (she wants everything done her way). This person makes herself feel so essential to others that it seems impossible for her to have any fun or to be away from her family for any length of time.

The perfect woman tends to overreact in most relationships. Her expectations put a high demand on all her relationships.

It is said, "We are more hurt by our expectations than by what people actually do to hurt us." The perfectionist wife has high expectations of her husband. She expects him to read her mind. She expects him to do tasks the way she would do them.

In a relationship this rationale takes away the other person's self-esteem. The husband can never live up to his wife's expectations. As the marriage progresses she chips away his self-esteem day after day. She criticizes what he does and how he does it; she always shows him a better way.

The husband withdraws. He becomes less involved in family happenings. He buries himself in his work, sleeps a lot, watches television, or absorbs himself in his favorite sport. He gets tired of hearing his wife criticizing him constantly. Sometimes he even turns to someone else who will listen to him and nurture him.

Bob and Alice had some guests on Sunday afternoon for a cookout. Alice asked Bob to put the steaks on the grill. First, she criticized him for not cutting the fat off the steak. Then she fussed about the coals. Then she kept commenting on the time he was taking to cook the steaks.

Their guests were getting uneasy. Bob tried to laugh it off and act like a little boy, but as the evening wore on it was easy to see the anger Alice was hiding because Bob was not living up to her expectations. Bob was becoming uneasy with her constant harping. By the end of the evening Bob and Alice were arguing and their guests were extremely uncomfortable. This shows just one way in which perfectionism can sabotage a relationship.

Coming under authority is another problem that confronts a perfectionist woman. Because of her "know-it-all" attitude, it is hard for her to believe that someone else can know as much as she does. This kind of woman may find it hard going in her marriage because she cannot come under God's divine order.

This carries over into her personal life to the extent that she rebels against God's divine plan for her own life.

The perfectionist woman struggles so long to stay on top of things, that when she does lose control, she tends to go "out of control." The principle of authority for the perfectionist woman not only hinders her relationships in her home, but also in the workplace. A manager told me she had an employee who was such a perfectionist that she was continually jealous of other workers. This led to much bitterness and resentment.

One day all the workers got together and gave the boss a nice card for "Bosses' Day." All the other folks in the office signed it "to our boss," but not perfectionist Pam. Her explanation was "I'd rather use the term friend instead of boss," denoting that she could not see her supervisor as her boss.

Perfectionist women are often impatient. They want things done not only their way, but done in their time, which is right now! This attitude makes it impossible to come under God's divine plan since He does things in His own timing. When people live in a family situation, or work with people, the time for things to get done is not always "right now."

Because the perfectionist woman overreacts when she gets hurt, and this is quite often, she often tries to resolve the problem by quitting her job, breaking off a friendship or by getting even. This constant anger-hurt syndrome continues to destroy her relationships - and this is sad.

By their very nature, perfectionists are strong-willed. Anna was one example of this type of personality. She sought counseling. She told her story. She and her husband lived in New York City with their two young sons. She was very unhappy. She begged her husband to move to Florida. He did not want to "uproot the family," so he refused.

After much nagging, and no budging on her husband's part, she finally went to Florida with her two boys. She found a house. Finally, her husband followed her down to the sunshine state.

Anna had always been a homemaker. Her husband could not find work so he took a job as a waiter in an exclusive country club. Anna was unsatisfied.

She wanted to go to school, so she began taking classes at the community college in her area. She blamed her husband for her failing the two classes she took, because he would not support her or help her. In fact, she said he hindered her.

She continued to nag her husband because they did not own their own home, and after twenty years of marriage had no savings and no insurance. He did not have a "decent job," she said. Everything was wrong.

Her husband could not stand the "fire" so he started hanging out at the country club after work and soon got involved with a young waitress.

Anna became even more heartsick. She was ready to leave him. Nothing else would do.

When asked by the counselor to consider waiting until she could develop some skills to get a better paying job to support herself and her children, she answered, "No way."

In this particular situation the counselor could easily see that Anna's "hurt" meant more to her than seeing that her children had a roof over their head or food on the table. As a perfectionist, she could only see the present and feel her pain. She was unable to see the "big picture." Anna could not focus on the broader perspective.

When a perfectionist woman nurtures her hurts, she may make rash decisions and sometimes unhealthy decisions. This adversely affects not only the individual but her entire family.

The perfectionist carries with her a lot of hostility. Her expectations are always high and are not always met, so she always feels let down. She has a hard time letting other people in her family take responsibility. She can always do the job better, faster or easier. She is always worn to a frazzle because she is always overloaded.

She expects other members of the family to clean up after themselves. When they don't, she fusses and does it for them. They always know that "dear ol' mom" will do it, so they never pick up their things. Thus, mom carries a lot of pent-up bitterness, resentment and anxiety. But rather than letting them know how she feels, she plays the martyr role.

Not letting others share in specific tasks around the home prevents mom from being a team player. She becomes a role model of the "Lone Ranger" type.

Insight into our perfectionist personalities can be corrective (as we will discuss in the next chapter). But it can also be a hazard.

A woman complained that her husband was irresponsible and failed to take the proper male leadership in the home. What she realized, after some introspection, was that she was so control-oriented that he could never discover how to lead her where she wanted to go, or to ask her to do what she wanted to do.

"Introspection is a process of investigating ourselves to find where we are at fault and to see what we can do about correcting our faults," writes Maurice Wagner, in his book, *Put It All Together*.[1] This process is difficult for all of us. It is even harder for the perfectionist.

We all have a built-in tendency to avoid accepting blame. It is also natural for us to hold onto our self-esteem while critically examining ourselves. We can easily lose all objectivity and blame ourselves excessively or distort facts so that we do not see our own responsibility in a particular matter.

Herein lies a dilemma: those who have good interpersonal relationships with others have little insecurity and can introspect easily. But those who have poor interpersonal relationships are often insecure and cannot introspect well. In fact, the poorer one's relationships are with others, the more one is inclined toward being defensive and insecure, and the less one can depend upon being reassured by others if one should find a fault in oneself.

Actually, we can all introspect better than we first think we can. If a woman thinks of herself as a sort of "it" instead of as a person of value, she will be devastated when she unveils a fault. This is compounded when she is a perfectionist.

Defective things are discarded; defective people are not. People who are not perfectionists find it easy to say, "No one is perfect." The perfectionist, however, is inbred with a different set of messages. But even with all of that, by the grace of God and by identifying with their friends who have overcome defects, perfectionists can build a perspective on the problem that they have discovered in themselves.

With their theme, "If I'm not perfect, then I'm nothing - I refuse to acknowledge any goodness in myself, for there will probably be a defect in it also. I can never be good, so why try?"- it takes introspection with *faith and grace* to overcome.

Introspection is looking at oneself critically. But, for a Christian, not *alone*. There is One who stands with her to reassure and give her hope that she can do the right thing. She can criticize herself and function in her own best interest. But she is not seeking insight simply in order to be a better person so she can glory in her improvement. She seeks rather to glorify God.

Thus the Christian woman can look within profitably, for she has a vital relationship with God which is supported by the matchless Word of God and the work of Christ on the Cross. She can hold onto this while seeking new insights into her own faults and know that God still loves her.

Insight is at work when we admit that we are growing. As long as we live, we expect to grow to higher plateaus of emotional maturation. This attitude helps to cancel the deadly effects of unrealistic idealization. Instead of being discouraged by some deficiency because the ideal fantasy of our own perfection was smashed, discovering a deficiency has a sense of challenge. If we never expect to get there, we will not be so devastated when we discover that we are not there yet. Yet there is a sense of accomplishment in the journey.[2]

Another attitude that will guide us in this time of introspection is to acknowledge our problem as our own, and not to blame someone or something else. We need to keep our mind on correction, not on rationalization, excuses or exaggeration. Our sins need to be dealt with. When we confess them as ours we are well on our way to healing from this disease called perfectionism. As someone has said, "God forgives sin, not excuses."

In guiding our attitudes when recovering from perfectionism, we must avoid comparing ourselves with others. When Peter attempted to compare himself with John, Jesus responded emphatically, "If I will that he tarry till I come [referring to His second coming], what is that to thee?" (John 21:23). We would do well to accept the attitude recommended by the Apostle Paul when he wrote to the Romans, "Whether we live, we live unto the Lord; and whether we die, we die unto the Lord: whether we live therefore, or die, we are the Lord's" (Rom. 14:8).

One very important attitude for the perfectionist to adopt is a daily commitment to God. This personal relationship with God establishes a sense of worth and well-being because we know His forgiveness and acceptance.

His ownership of our lives gives Him the right to guide our minds in this self-evaluation, because His goals are always good and right. Here, the ministry of the Holy Spirit convicts us of sin and makes us into the very image of Christ. We can more readily accept our deficiencies when we know we have a loving, heavenly Father pointing them out to us for our own good and for His glory.

Dale Carnegie once said, "You can make more friends in two months by becoming interested in other people than you can in two years by trying to get other people interested in you."

I asked a group of students what they thought a good definition of a perfect woman was. Without a moment's hesitation, one student replied, "No matter how hard you try to please them, or how much you do for them, they never appreciate your efforts."

Perfectionists have a hard time compromising. You can't please them if the task or job isn't done their way. Compromise is a proven tool in being able to get along with difficult people. Yet some individuals resist using it because, underneath, they'd really like to have their own way.

Think of a person with whom you have a problem right now. Is there some concession you could offer that you have been unwilling to give in the past? Could you move across the center barrier onto their side? They may not deserve it - and yes, you might lose face, but remember the Lord's own words in Matthew 5:9: "Blessed are the peacemakers: for they shall be called the children of God."

Florence Littauer, in her book, *How to Get Along with Difficult People*, tells the story of Marita who at the age of thirteen lived in the era of tie-dyed T-shirts and frayed jeans. Littauer writes:

> Even though I had grown up in the Depression and had no money for clothes, I had never dressed this poorly. One day I

58

saw her out in the driveway rubbing the hems of her new jeans with dirt and rocks. I was aghast at her ruining these pants I had just paid for and ran out to tell her so. She continued to grind on as I recounted my soap opera of childhood deprivation in the driveway. As I concluded without having moved her to tears of repentance, I asked why she was wrecking her new jeans. She replied without looking up, "You can't wear new ones."

"Why not?"

"You just can't, so I'm messing them up to make them look old." Such total loss of logic! How could it be the style to ruin new clothes?

Each morning as she would leave for school I would stare at her and sigh, "My daughter looking like that." There she'd stand in her father's old T-shirt, tie-dyed with big blue spots and streaks. Fit for a duster, I thought. And those jeans - so low-slung I feared if she took a deep breath they'd drop off her rear. But where would they go? They were so tight and stiff they couldn't move. The frayed bottoms, helped by the rocks, had strings that dragged behind her as she walked.

One day after she had left for school, it was as if the Lord got my attention and said, "Do you realize what your last words are to Marita each morning? 'My daughter looking like that.' When she gets to school and her friends talk about their old-fashioned mothers who complain all the time, she'll have your constant comments to contribute. Have you ever looked at the other girls in junior high? Why not give them a glance."

I drove over to pick her up that day and observed that many of the other girls looked worse. On the way home I mentioned how I had overreacted to her ruining her jeans. I offered a compromise: "From now on you can wear anything you want to school and with your friends, and I won't bug you about it."

"That'll be a relief."

"But when I take you out with me to church or shopping or to my friends, I'd like you to dress in something you know I like without my having to say a word."

She thought about it.

Then I added, "That means you get 95 percent your way and I get 5 percent for me. What do you think?"

She got a twinkle in her eye as she put out her hand and shook mine. "Mother, you've got yourself a deal!"

From then on I gave her a happy farewell in the morning and didn't bug her about her clothes. When I took her out with me, she dressed properly without fussing. We had ourselves a deal![3]

Florence Littauer goes on to say that within the year, her daughter went from those huge, ugly T-shirts to pretty ones, and the next year into blouses, sweaters, and skirts. By her senior year in high school she dressed like a model and she's looked that way ever since. Now she teaches other women how to dress and has written *Shades of Beauty: The Color Coordinated Woman.*[4]

Again, as I have stated before, it is hard to please a perfectionist. For example, one woman put it this way:

From the time I was a child I remember seeking my mother's approval. I always did well in everything I tackled, and I knew enough not to attempt sports, art, or music because I had no talent in these areas. My mind could learn the rules, principles, or keyboard, but my body wouldn't cooperate. My mother, a violin and cello teacher, was disappointed that I couldn't even hold the bow correctly, so I set out to excel where I could. I got good grades and hoped that Mother would praise me.

Once when I asked her why she didn't tell other people how well I was doing in school after Peggy's mother had bragged about her, she replied, "You never know when you'll have to eat your words."

Throughout life I've tried to pull a compliment out of Mother, but, while she was never negative, she hung in at neutral. One day within the past year I came home after a frustrating visit. I'd shown Mother my exciting schedule of speaking, including a European trip, a Canadian retreat, and an Alaskan cruise. Her response was, "It's amazing you're so busy considering what you do is something nobody needs."[5]

Since a perfectionist is a rigid person, it is not too difficult to see why she has so much difficulty in maintaining a wholesome relationship. Dwight Carlson, in his book *Run and Not Be Weary* describes a rigid person as one who is poured into a mold of her own making or one made by others. Her life is constricted, inhibited in growth and expression.[6]

Literally, rigid means "to be stiff" and "to be right." It also means something is inflexible, unyielding, firm or severe. Carlson goes on to say that the rigid woman lacks teachability, pliability, openness of heart, mind and ideas.

Rigidity is caused primarily by compulsive impulses from within or by legalistic requirements imposed from without. Both causes tie in with the perfectionist personality as we have already discussed. The compulsive woman tends to be formal, meticulous, overly inhibited, self-doubting and fastidious. She is often compelled by forces from within, forces that she does not understand. She performs activities which she would rather not undertake. This includes anything from very mild activity to compulsive neurosis.

In a housewife, this characteristic can be quite difficult for a husband and children. For example, observe the housewife who prides herself in having everything just right. On a given evening, whether through poor planning, or unexpected interruptions, she has four hours of work to do and only two hours before guests arrive.

If she cannot redefine her priorities and decide what can and must be done in the two hours, she is liable to be very frustrated and anxious. She may enter such a state of panic that she does not properly use the time she does have and may even ruin the evening for everyone involved, causing much embarrassment to her husband.[7]

As Charlie Shedd points out in *Time for All Things*, all of us face "divine interruptions" which can throw a monkey wrench into our plans if we are rigid and compulsive. Sometimes these divine interruptions are our greatest potential opportunities, when seen in light of the big picture. Wives who cannot reevaluate and place new priorities when these situations arise will become shackled by their own lock and chain. This leads to all kinds of problems, both personally and in her married life.

Some say that the causes of these uninvited internal compulsive behavior patterns often stem from repressed and unconscious bitterness, resentment, guilt, anxiety or insecurity. These may have originated years earlier in a person's life. Knowing this, we must resolve the deep internal conflicts responsible for this behavior. The last chapter explores this subject. But, before going further, two additional thoughts concerning perfectionists need to be considered, namely, problems in relationships caused by judgmental attitudes and people pleasers.

Many perfectionists are prone to being judgmental. The Bible tells why this is so: "Therefore you have no excuse, O man, whoever you are, when you judge another; for in passing judgement upon him you condemn yourself, because you, the judge, are doing the very same things," (Rom. 2:1). In Christ's example of judging one's brother (see Matt.7), both were afflicted with the same problem - wood in the eye. The brother with the larger piece failed to realize his own need (it was close to his blind spot). Nevertheless, he was more ready to see it in his brother and to want to help him with his problem.[8]

We can see how this kind of negativism within a marriage could play havoc with the growth and development of an intimate relationship. In this vein, the woman who judges her husband or children is (consciously or unconsciously) trying to keep them from noticing her flaws. This critical attitude often comes from feelings of inferiority. Pointing out flaws in others is a perfectionist woman's attempt to build herself up in her own eyes and in the eyes of others.

This does not happen, though; instead, it leads to the souring of relationships.

Sometimes this finding fault with others is nothing more than a bad habit because so many ears are ready to listen. Not only that, but it can prevent a wife or mother from getting involved in the positive endeavors others advocate. Taking a positive action is work and may leave one open to criticism of oneself.

This leads to the final idea that we want to deal with in this chapter - that of the people-pleasing perfectionist personality.

Very few people that I know are happy about being criticized. In other words, the healthiest of us suffer from a tremendous desire to please, to be understood and to be accepted by others. However, for some people the primary purpose in life is to please people. This motivation is based not on love for others but on self-love.[9]   It is an unhealthy desire to gain favor, praise, understanding and love for themselves. Therefore, they are highly self-centered.

So these people-pleasers feel they must have the approval of others, regardless of the cost. Too often, the cost is the joy of an intimate relationship.

The people pleaser does not know her own mind because she is so involved in trying to figure out what her friends are thinking. This forces her to continually wear a mask.

Ironic as it may seem, she usually keeps people at arm's length. She wants admirers but at a distance. This includes her family, because she fears that closeness will expose her. This robs her of close friendships and close relationships with her own family because the closer people get, the more likely they will come to see behind her mask of   self-centeredness   and   self-love.

Often legitimate family needs, and even her own needs, will go ignored as she frantically tries to impress her more distant audience. If she continues trying to please people, she will never know God's will, nor His potential for her.

Jesus said, "How on earth can you believe (have faith) while you are forever looking for one another's approval and not for the glory that comes from the one God?" (John 5:44, Phillips).

The Apostle Paul - in dealing with the various relationships of husband, wife, child, parent, employer and employee - makes this point, "Not with eye-service, as men-pleasers; but as the servants of Christ, doing the will of God from the heart; With good will doing service as to the Lord, and not to men: Knowing that whatsoever good thing any man doeth, the same shall he receive of the Lord, whether he be bond or free," (Eph. 6:6-8).

Because women who are people-pleasers have seldom been involved in wholesome, loving, giving relationships, they may in the end lose everything - God, family and all their coveted admirers. An example of this is found in the Bible with Balaam.

The prophet Balaam communicated with God. He was advised by God not to return with King Balak's honored men. But the people pressed him and, with the allure of personal gain, he yielded. The result was a trouble-filled trip. Both God and King Balak were angry at him. His acts cost him his life (Num. 22-24, 31).

If the people-pleasing perfectionist can go God's way, seeking Him above all else, she can have true love and acceptance - first from God, then from significant others in her life and even from herself. A woman who seeks to please God will, in fact, please many others. This includes pleasing her most cherished family, which will be an incidental result, rather than a primary motivating factor.

This will be addressed in the final chapter - The Perfect Woman: "God" Controlled.

1. Maurice E. Wagner, Ph.D., *Put It All Together* (Grand Rapids: Zondervan Publishing House, 1974), p. 135.

2. Ibid., p. 40.

3. Florence Littauer, *How to Get Along with Difficult People* (Eugene: Harvest House Publishers, 1984), p. 150.

4. Ibid.

5. Ibid., p. 160.

6. Dwight Carlson, *Run and Not Be Weary* (Old Tappan: Fleming H. Revell Company, 1974), p. 113.

7. Ibid., p. 114.

8. Ibid., p. 128.

9. Ibid., p. 133.

4
The Perfect Woman: "God" Controlled

Vine's Expository Dictionary of New Testament Words defines sin (*harmatia*) as missing the mark, denoting an act or continual practice of disobedience to Divine law. Vine also defines repentance (*metanoia*) as changing one's mind in regard to sin and evil.

Sin separates us from God; repentance leads to reconciliation. Perfectionism is a condition of self-centered separation between a person and God that leads to alienation from other people as well.

Throughout the Bible, there is evidence of God's people not hearing or seeing. When Moses went up on the mountain for forty days, the people quickly "forgot" and broke their covenant, even at the risk of death, as if the covenant had never existed. As a result, God was ready to destroy them. At Moses' urging and intercession, the people were saved from being "blotted out" (Exod. 32).

Isaiah spoke of the people's hearing but not understanding, and seeing but not perceiving. He intimated that if they could somehow hear and see the truth, and understand, they could be healed (Isa. 6:9f.). It was as though someone had put an evil wall between the eyes and ears of the people. At times, they were spiritually deaf and blind, yet did not even know it.

In the New Testament, Jesus used parables to get around this wall of denial that had been built up. This enabled people to see and hear the truth and to be healed (Matt. 13:13). He said to His disciples, in obvious irritation, "Having eyes do you not see, and having ears do you not hear? And do you not remember?" (Mark 8:18).

We need to remember Paul's confessed struggle with abiding sin and his own statement of this confusing problem of denial's relation to sin after years of following Christ:

I do not understand my own actions. For I do not do what I want, but I do the very thing I hate.... So then it is no longer I that do it, but sin which dwells within me...I can will what is right, but I cannot do it. For I do not do the good I want, but the evil I do not want is what I do. Now if I do what I do not want, it is no longer I that do it, but sin which dwells within me (Rom. 7:15-20).

A number of fine Christian people have assumed that because God overcame sin they need no longer concern themselves with it. But a close look at the New Testament shows that, although sin may have been overcome at its core, each of us still must battle with our own sin and with the disease that it started and maintains in the world today.

Many perfectionists often cloak their sin in respectability - "helping" and even what they call "ministry." Because of this attitude of "always being right," they want things done their way.

They seem to offer people love and attention, when in fact they are using them for their own self-satisfaction. For example, a woman may take on more and more tasks or responsibilities in order to have things done her way. Her colleagues may think she is wonderful for being so helpful. But sooner or later she will become resentful and bitter, and cause discomfort and disease within the church or in the organization in which she is working.

"For all have sinned, and come short of the glory of God," writes the Apostle Paul to the Romans (Rom. 3:23). John adds to the revelation of God's Word by writing, "If we say we have no sin, we deceive ourselves, and the truth is not in us" (1 John 1:8). This indicates that we, in and of ourselves, cannot even see, much less change, without God. We are powerless to heal ourselves.

Our selfishness, perfectionism and desire to always be right in our family, vocational life and other relationships lead us to be lonely, resentful and angry. We deviously work out our self-centered desires by denying that we are conscious of our desire to control other people and to take God's place in our small circle of influence. We live in a delusion of righteousness while we cause havoc in the lives of others.

In overcoming the sins of perfectionism we realize how miserable and confused we are. Paul described his confusing dilemma this way: "I of myself serve the law of God with my mind, but with my flesh [the urgent, unconscious part] I serve the law of sin" (Rom. 7:25). In this same context, Paul cries the same thing we do when we see our powerlessness to make things right on our own, "Wretched man that I am! Who will deliver me from this body of death?" (Rom. 7:24). When we become sick and tired of confusion, anxiety and a feeling of being burned out, we realize that we are powerless to fix life up for ourselves and for other people.

Keith Miller quotes another writer:

Each person is like an actor who wants to run the whole show; is forever trying to manage the lights, the ballet, the scenery and the rest of the players in his own way. If his arrangements would only stay put, if only people would do as he wishes, the show would be great. Everybody, including himself, would be pleased. Life would be wonderful. In trying to make these arrangements our actor may sometimes be quite virtuous. He (or she) may be kind, considerate, patient, generous; even modest and self-sacrificing. On the other hand, he may be mean, egotistical, selfish and dishonest. But as with most humans, he is likely to have varied traits.

What usually happens? The show doesn't come off very well. He begins to think life doesn't treat him right. He decides to exert himself more. He becomes, on the next occasion, still more demanding or gracious, as the case may be. Still the play does not suit him. Admitting he may be somewhat at fault, he is sure that other people are more to blame. He becomes angry, indignant, self-pitying. What is his basic trouble? Is he not really a self seeker even when trying to be kind? Is he not a victim of the delusion that he can wrest satisfaction and happiness out of this world if he only manages well? Is it not evident to all the rest of the players that these are the things he wants? And do not his actions make each of them wish to retaliate, snatching all they can get out of the show? Is he not, even in his best moments, a producer of confusion rather than harmony?[1]

So, as we begin to see what is happening in lives, we come to realize that *the perfect woman's flaw* is to go on her own power and not *God's* power. In and of ourselves, we do not have the power to defeat this perfectionist thinking. When we are willing to give up control of our life and that of others, when we completely surrender, then God's power can overcome the sin of perfectionism in our lives.

The perfect woman has to become aware of her perfectionist attitude. This awareness helps her to see her controlling attitude and her failing relationships. In putting this perfect attitude in the center of our living, it becomes an idol, thus replacing God as the security and center of our lives.

Quoting again from Keith Miller in his book, *Sin*, he writes:

> As long as things are going well in the area of our sin-security, we feel important and in control. But sooner or later, putting something or someone in the center of one's life, where only God belongs, leads a sensitive person to the end of his or her rope. Evidently nothing will give us the safety and power of God in our lives, except God. When we over focus our lives upon anything other than God, sooner or later we spoil it, and it will fail us. For, in fact, we are not in control of life, and no thing or person can meet our deepest needs for security and fulfillment.[2]

For a woman who has spent her entire life as the perfect woman, realizing her powerlessness may come in the form of a personal crisis. A rush of shame and fear may come when she realizes that she doesn't have the power to fix things up or to hide the problem.

For example, Noreen came into a counselor's office crying and filled with hurt, pain and confu-

77

sion. Her husband of twenty-two years had just walked out on her and was living with some "bimbo." He was furious with Noreen and blamed her for his weakness.

As Noreen shared her story, she realized that her husband was born into a family of alcoholic parents and so he came from a dysfunctional family. He never rebelled as a child or teenager because he didn't have anyone to rebel against. His parents had no restrictions.

When he married Noreen she was a churchgoing woman and encouraged him to go. She was the "perfect little wife," but treated him as though he were a child. She ran the household and told him what he could and could not do.

One day he rebelled against her authority and perfectionist personality. It took this crisis for Noreen to look inside herself. She surrendered her will to God's will. With God in control, she began to change.

All these years she had a big ego, but low self-esteem. Her self-esteem went down even further when her husband blamed her for all his problems.

At this low ebb she could see her shortcomings and her sin of perfectionism. As Noreen began to change and to forgive her husband, he began to see her in a different light and responded to her forgiveness. But more than that, he responded to

her putting God first in her life. In Matthew 6:30-
34 we find the words of Christ: "Seek ye first the
Kingdom of God and all these things shall be
added unto you."

Noreen started to seek the King. She gave up
her control and, in Him, found that "all things hold
together" (Col. 1:17, RSV). Noreen and her
husband have a long way to go for their recovery,
but they are on the right path. Thus, it took a
personal crisis for God to get her attention and to
work in her heart.

It's interesting how it takes some individuals
so much pain - at a crisis point they decide that
whatever the cost, they have to change something
because their anger is too much.

Leighton Ford, Billy Graham's brother-in-law,
has said "God loves us just the way we are, but he
loves us too much to let us stay that way."

It may take a personal crisis for the sin of
perfection to be revealed. Once admitted and
acknowledged, then the person has the choice of
staying the way she is, with emotional pain, or
admitting her sin to God and giving up her own
control to God. Surrendering to God will give one
a relaxed mental attitude, thus allowing other
people to be who they are.

Everyone seems to always cry out to have their
own way. Everyone has his or her own agenda.

But acknowledging one's perfectionism will help overcome the flaw of a woman being in control, rather than allowing God to be in control.

Even though they think they are in control, most perfectionists are out of control. So how can they control others?

Somewhere during our childhood we think we can control other people. We start as small children trying to manipulate our parents. As we grow older our parents try to control us and thus the vicious cycle begins. Our assumed right to change other people - even for their own good - is a sin-inspired illusion.

Thomas Merton said that the beginning of love is to let those we love be perfectly themselves, and not to twist them to fit our own image. Otherwise we love only the reflection of ourselves we find in them.

Under full sail I had set out on a course to "make my family happy," but I couldn't see that I was trying to make them behave as I would, to have the happiness I would have wanted were I in their shoes. Fortunately they wanted to live their own lives and find the happiness God put in their own imaginations.

To decide to give control of our lives to God is only a step. Surrendering our wills to God is a living process. We take one situation at a time, as we discover God's will in our lives and confront the sin of perfectionism. As we pray we tell God we tried to take His place and in so doing hurt the people we want to love because of our intense, perfect self-centeredness. We need to ask for His forgiveness. We must surrender our will to Him daily, hour by hour, moment by moment.

In order for us to become the person God wants us to be we must realize that these behavior and thought patterns have been with us since we were children. We put away childish things - yet become like a child again before God in order to rid ourselves of this defect of character that causes us to remain in the delusion of being the center and in control.

In his book, *Sin*, Keith Miller wrote, "Someone asked me if I thought I could trust God with my life for one day only. I said, 'Of course.' He told me that was all I ever had to do, because today is the only real time there is." Can you trust God for twenty-four hours? Someone has said, "We are so busy living in the past, organizing the present and living in the future, that we are not living in the moment."[3]

Since we unconsciously need to control those around us in order to make us happy (or think we are making them happy) we overlook God's plan.

Allowing God to control our lives begins before our feet hit the floor each morning. Waking up with Him on our mind, we pray and thank Him for the night of rest and surrender our will to Him for the rest of that day. We must talk with God constantly as is indicated for those of us who are God's children in 1 Thessalonians 5:17, "Pray without ceasing." You must tell God what you are feeling and thinking. When you are in relationships and you pray what you are feeling, God can give you wisdom on how to handle the situation.

Suppose your husband just came in and started rearranging his office that is housed in the back bedroom. He hasn't said a word to you about it. He simply starts shuffling papers and fussing around.

He's thinking that this is his office and he can do whatever he pleases. On the other hand, *you* are thinking, "What's going on? What is he doing? Why doesn't he wait till I can help him?"

Then you say to him, "Don't move that furniture. Don't put those papers in that file."

You start feeling angry. First of all he didn't share his intentions with you. He didn't invite you into his world, so to speak. Secondly, he's not doing it your way.

The anger mounts - the perfectionist within raises its ugly head.

Stop! Pray! Tell God you are angry. Tell God that you admit you want things done your way.

Tell God you are hurt because your husband didn't share with you his decision to rearrange the office.

Perfectionists want things done right, and right is their way of doing things.

When you express your feelings to God and allow yourself to experience the feelings you have, you can find relief from anger and pain. When you pray to God about your anger, you begin to see a new kind of control. This new control begins when you decide to change your own life. You can then learn not to always overreact in your relationships.

For you to not have to play God brings a great sense of release.

Wives who can help their loved ones by listening, nurturing and allowing them to choose their own actions, will be the helpmeets God designed them to be.

If our purpose in praying to God is not to get what we want, but to discern His will for our relationships and daily life, then we will begin to overcome this perfectionist attitude. It is through this process of praying about our feelings that we get insights into how to best love the people with whom we live and deal with daily. When we pray to God about our feelings, He can teach us to have an attitude of gratitude.

Perfectionists tend to criticize and complain. But when God is the center of your life you tend to be more serene and peaceful. You experience inner joy and peace.

The following is used by permission of a woman in a counseling situation, who said:

> I have always been a perfectionist, but didn't realize it until some unexpected occurrences happened in my life, primarily within my marriage of fifteen years. I now consider myself a recovering perfectionist, working hard at changing my perfectionist behaviors. This change has not been easy for me, however, and probably never would have occurred had I not experienced a great deal of pain and hurt (which I have learned is a major cause of a person to develop the desire to change).
>
> Early in my marriage I was domineering and demanding, setting high expectations not only for myself, but for my husband and children as well. Consequently, my husband worked hard to meet my expectations, but not without building up resentment and fear within himself towards me throughout those early years. It was not until my husband told me one day that he had been unhappy for a long time and was actually

afraid of me that I began taking a closer look at myself and my behavior. I had been spending all those years looking for ways to change him rather than accept him.

Up until this time, I thought I was the model wife, giving support and encouragement to my husband in his career, providing a clean house and well-balanced meals, assuming much of the day-to-day responsibilities such as the children's activities and family finances, taking good care of myself, and socializing with friends and relatives. In fact, if you would have asked me, I would have told you we had the "perfect" marriage. So, of course, I was devastated to hear the news of his being unhappy. However, the worst news was yet to follow. After seemingly rebuilding our relationship and even constructing a beautiful new home, my world was shattered when, a few years later, my husband voiced his unhappiness once again. This time, however, was different - another woman was involved. I could hardly believe it, even after his admission. You see, we are Christians. We had been active in service, having served as youth counselors, Sunday school teachers, and youth Bible study leaders. We had even attended a Bible study ourselves for the past five years. How could this happen to us? What went wrong this time?

Without explaining the agonizing emotional trauma experienced and the details of the five months of separation, I can tell you that God opened my eyes to what He means by unconditional love as explained in 1 Corinthians 13. It was through His love for me and my husband that we were able to reunite. Counseling, reading and much prayer were essential activities that enabled me to change - to forgive, to accept, to love unconditionally.

One of the hardest things I did while my husband and I were separated was to turn all the financial responsibilities over to my husband. It was frightening because people were saying that I should protect my financial position. But, part of our marital problems stemmed from the fact that I had assumed too much responsibility and there was very little participation on my husband's part concerning family responsibility. I have learned that it is important for him to be a contributor. He, too, needs to feel needed. This is still a difficult situation for me because my husband is not the best bookkeeper (we have paid several late payment charges and have overdrawn our checking account). I know contributing and assuming more responsibility is more important and God has removed much of my worry concerning the finances and any desire to control them. When you have come so close to having your family destroyed, even the finances seem unimportant.

Another change that has occurred is that I no longer feel that our home must be spotless all the time. We used to spend just about every Saturday cleaning (notice I said "we"). However, after my husband voiced how much he resented that routine, I made some adjustments. When my husband stated that he felt that "our house" and its appearance was more important to me than "our home," I began making some changes there as well. For instance, I began to work on one room or so every day so that everything wouldn't have to be done in one day. Eventually, I hired someone to help me. I simply changed priorities and gave my family attention rather than my household chores. In fact, if you visited me now during the week, you'd probably even find my bed unmade. But, we certainly enjoy family activities on the weekends now.

Through this experience, I have indeed learned so much about myself, God's love and steadfastness, the real meaning of faith and hope, and the fragility of the marriage relationship. Change does not come easy and takes consistent effort, but I like myself more than I ever have and am discovering a fun-filled, easy-going spirit that worries less, has fewer expectations, and is more accepting and less critical.

Mimi Boynton was kind enough to share her experience in the May, 1989 issue of *These Days*. Her doctor told her that she had scarlet fever and prescribed one week of complete bed rest. Even though her doctor knew she had four children under the age of six, he said, "You only have one heart. Go home and go to bed."

She thought to herself, "Now isn't that just like a man? Doesn't he know that mothers are indispensable?"

But providentially for her family a blizzard closed schools for an entire week. It was a time of discovery. Her twelve-year-old son proved able to prepare simple meals, and he diapered and fed the baby expertly. He learned how to operate the washer and bullied his younger brother Allen into hanging wash in the basement while standing on a chair.

Mimi discovered that the little girls could put away folded laundry neatly, and her daughter Hannah knew to whom each article belonged. Baby Douglas cooperated by taking extra-long naps. It was a week of minor miracles, a week of love in action.

Did all the week go smoothly? Not exactly! Sometimes the children bickered and fussed. But Mimi resolutely turned a deaf ear and stayed in bed.

The family emerged from the week feeling loving, competent and self-confident. Mimi learned one of life's major lessons: No one is indispensable, not even a mother. "Whatever you are doing, put your heart into it, as if you were doing it for the Lord and not for men" (Col. 3:23, NEB).

It is always good to learn about those in the process of overcoming a diseased area of their lives. Living with perfectionists can be a challenge but even that can work out for good. For example, a young lady in her mid-twenties writes:

Growing up with a perfectionist mother was not easy for me. As a little girl my mom molded me into a "perfect" child, who always obeyed her and pleased her. But as I

grew into my own selfhood, it seemed to me
that my mother could not let go. She still
tried to shape me into being as she was -
"perfect, good, and right." It became harder
as I grew into my adolescent years, because
I struggled to be that "perfect child" and
"perfect woman" I thought my mother
wanted me to be. All I ever wanted was her
love and approval, but what I got from her
did not seem like love. An illustration of
this occurred when I was in the fifth grade
and it had to do with my hair. I had long,
blond, curly hair that took a lot of care, but
guess who did it for me? Yes, my mother.
She did it her way and did not teach me how
to make it look the way she wanted it to
look. So the times I did do my own hair, it
did not satisfy her and so she would redo it
her way. Finally, one day she said, "If you
can't keep your hair looking good, we'll
have to cut it short." As I remember, I
finally persuaded her to let me have it cut
short, thinking that would please her, or it
may have been somewhat out of rebellion.
At any rate, this did not work out either,
because my hair kept getting oily and just
looked horribly and would not do right. I
just could not seem to keep it the way mom

wanted it to look and it became an issue between us that made me not feel loved for the way I was.

I didn't want to be just like her, although ironically I admired her. I wanted my mother to accept me for who I was, flaws and all.

However, my mother kept trying to control me throughout my teenage years, at least that is how I felt. So my love for her turned into rage when I realized that I wasn't perfect after all. I just couldn't please my mother all of the time and still feel free to be myself. The independence inside of me won out - if I couldn't be mommie's "perfect little girl," then I could be a "perfect failure."

Somehow people tend to blame adolescent development for rebelliousness. But as I reflect on my own experience, during that time I knew I wanted to be my own person. I wanted to be a woman different from my mother and yet the same. I did not want to be forced into perfection. However, it seemed to me that mother did not want me to grow into womanhood, and also wanted to make decisions for me and not let me make my own. I felt like she wanted me to be the compliant child so that she could control me.

I resisted my mother's domination over me for quite a few years, at least until my early twenties. Then there came a point in my life when I wanted to regress into that "little girl" syndrome again, where everything was safe from the pressures of the world. I wanted my independence, yet there was something inside me that wanted to scream out for my parent's protection. I began to starve myself symbolically in order to lose my womanhood I had once desperately fought for. And now seemingly, after I had tasted that independence, I had failed my mother once again. It was time for me to regain the innocence of my childhood. My rage and anger was no longer on my mom who was so "perfect," but turned in towards myself. So there I was an adult who was losing her womanly body just to become the "perfect girl" my mother always wanted me to be, or so I thought.

Through therapy I blossomed into womanhood again, except this time my mother was living in another state where her control was by her haunting words in my mind. Slowly, I began to take on responsibility for myself and my own actions. As I grew, I knew I would not be faultless, but I was free to be me. Ironically, my mother was recovering from her "perfectionism" about the same time. So she also became aware of her high expectations of me. I had my own expectations which I felt free to express. So through the past several years my mom and I have grown to accept and love one another as we once did when I was a small child. This time we are adults who accept each other - flaws and all. This pleases us both.

Still another lady writes:

I've always known I wasn't perfect. Never wanted to be. I thought I knew the definition of a perfectionist, but I didn't. I've been pushing to make things just right, rarely turning control over to God.

For many years while affiliated with my last husband, I felt as though his infidelity was directly related to me not being "good enough." I was continually trying to improve my physical appearance while accepting more and more responsibility for the relationship. Creating this perfect image which could not be equalled (everything for everybody) was so important to me that I lost my inner self.

The image was comprised of everything I could exhibit some sort of control over...appearance, attitude, children, home, business, husband, activities. That still was not enough.

Through God's guidance I found truth and wisdom and started to regain the moral balance I once operated my life by.

As I look back now I see how crazy and off balance my thinking was. Not only was this a life of a compulsive perfectionist, but one based on material things rather than spiritual.

Whenever I start to feel these tendencies toward perfectionism starting to overtake the balance in my present life, the new me says, "Lighten-up, let go and let God!" You see, I'm my own worst critic and I think that many times what I demand of myself is much more complicated and tedious than what God expects from me.

Perfect to me means *complete* or *total*, not missing a piece. I never had the desire to be flawless or exact as many people define perfection.

Coordinating everything to perfection has been my standard for many years. Just as perfect is an illusion, the illusion of being in total control has been a way of life for me for many years. As the expression goes, "I don't like to miss a trick." Through the years I have set standards for myself based on the way I was raised. As a young person living in a dysfunctional household my perception of balance was distorted. Unrealistic, superficial standards were imposed upon my life. I generally did not try to be the best at anything, but rather to do everything.

Balance is what appeals to me now. Taking responsibility for my life, yet relinquishing the desire to control others.

Georgia Witkin, Ph.D., a clinical psychologist and author of *Quick Fixes and Small Comforts*, writes "Most women are raised to please other people and to take care of them."[4] In addition, Witkin writes that women "seem to have a higher sensitivity than men to verbal cues, and consequently we're more likely to hear other people's needs and listen for their approval than men are."[5]

Trying to appear "good" seems to be a female preoccupation, but good-girlism is not necessarily all self-sacrifice and deception.

Kept in perspective, good-girl characteristics can be positive: A neat, ordered desk makes for more organized thinking; politeness and sensitivity to other people makes life more pleasant. The trick is to know when we are making the choice to behave like good girls and when we feel we are being coerced.

There has been a discernible movement recently toward coercing women into good-girl behavior. Witness the astonishing array of books for women - and often by women - about how to behave in a way that pleases men. For example, Toni Grant, Ph.D., in her book *Being a Woman*, advises a woman to cultivate the mystique of the Madonna, to keep her feelings to herself and, when she does speak, to speak softly.[6]

A proliferation of magazine articles encouraging women not to be open about their sexual needs, and a kind of gleeful newspaper coverage of career women leaving their jobs to devote themselves to home and children, contribute to the notion that good girlism is alive and well and thriving among us.

"It is true that our conservative climate does give more approval to those women who are choosing traditional good-girl roles," says Dr. Symonds, assistant clinical professor of psychiatry at New York University School of Medicine.[7]

But even those women who have chosen less traditional female roles do not escape the pressure to be "good." "Women working outside the home often translated the myth that they could have it all so they could *be* it all," says Dr. Witkin. "We women still have a hard time recognizing that we can't be everything to everyone. In trying to be good, we gave up none of our old roles when we took on new ones."[8]

If the image of the superwoman is our modern version of the good girl -the woman who can do it all so well that she pleases everyone - then rejection of that role might indicate that women are no longer trying to be good girls. But "women haven't stopped trying to be perfect," says Witkin.[9]

Ash DeLorenzo, trend director at Brain Reserve, Inc., a marketing consulting firm in New York City, agrees. "Women have not rejected the myth of the superwoman. Trends show, for example, that despite the fact that there are more women than ever in the work force, men are not taking on more of the housework."[10]

A twenty-nine-year-old public defender says she kept up a seamless good-girl performance throughout high school, entering her rebellion as soon as she left home. "I was always a good student, but because I felt it was even more important to be a good girl I made sure my academic skills didn't threaten anyone," she says. "I studied hard, but assiduously avoided any original thought. By the time I got to college, I'd managed to lower my IQ by several points at least."

She decided that betraying her gift of a good mind in order to "win some kind of popularity contest" made absolutely no sense. "Rather than retard myself to please the boys who felt threatened by my brains, I chose to date only brainy boys who welcomed the competition. Of course, that meant I didn't really get to date much until my second year of law school, but it also meant I didn't have to lie about my ambitions and, finally, that I didn't have to leave the plum jobs for someone else."[11]

"Self-sacrifice - leaving the plum jobs or the last cookie on the plate for someone else - is just one of the characteristics of the grown-up good girl," writes Jean Gonick in a recent article in *Self* magazine.[12] She continues, "The good girl fears fun and spontaneity. To maintain control, good girls need to impose rigidity on themselves and on those around them. Good girls tend to see the world as they did when they actually were little girls - with a child's underdeveloped, black-and-white sense of morality. Their enemies are the Bad People, their friends are the Good People. Terrified that those who truly know them will reject and abandon them, good girls have no choice but to please, serve and suppress, as best they can, their anger and disappointment."[13]

Symonds says, "The good girl develops indirect ways of expressing her anger and often becomes depressed. She expects others to take care of her in return for what she's done for them."[14]

Wanting your approval, the good girl will drive you to the airport whenever you ask her to do so. But being human (even "bad") underneath it all, she's angry at you for accepting the ride and can't entirely hide her resentment. The good girl in the extreme believes, on some very basic level, that she who sets out matching placemats and napkins is superior to one who does not. But regardless of her immaculate house and wardrobe, she is not a person to envy.[15]

Thus, once again, we come full circle to the "goodness" of the "good girl," yet the good girl is out of control. It is only when realizing that her strength comes from God, that she can be "God controlled."

The story of Samson's strength in the sixteenth chapter of Judges provides us with a great reminder that we must remember our source of strength and our gifts. Each of us has failed God at some time. Fortunately for the perfect woman, the God who honored the last prayer of Samson is always anxious to bring us back from disobedience.

"How can a holy God use an unholy people to do holy work?" asked Donald Baker, author of *A Fresh New Look At God.* "Before answering that we should probably remind ourselves that God has no other kind of people available."

"The answer," added Baker, "is *grace.*"

The perfect woman must come to God in her weakness and He will come to her in strength. The joy of forgiveness and the opportunity for future obedience await the truly repentant.

Perfectionism is a sin. It hinders relationships and our faith in God.

All of us, whether heroes or ordinary people, have flaws. Yet when we put ourselves at God's disposal, weakness and all, He will readily display His power through us - thus we are *God controlled*.

The following diagram indicates the tendency of a "perfectionist personality" to move in a downward thrust which usually leads to a poor relationship with others. An "awareness" of this perfectionist personality on the part of an individual, with a desire to change, results in becoming God controlled.

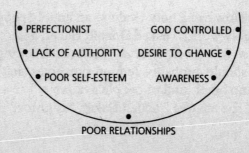

- PERFECTIONIST   GOD CONTROLLED -
- LACK OF AUTHORITY   DESIRE TO CHANGE -
- POOR SELF-ESTEEM   AWARENESS -

POOR RELATIONSHIPS

This brings about the biblical idea of the "perfect child of God" - one who comes under the authority of God and develops a good self-esteem, and thus enjoys a healthy relationship with God and with others.

1. J. Keith Miller, *Sin: Overcoming the Ultimate Deadly Addiction* (San Francisco: Harper & Row, Publishers, 1987), p. 108.

2. Ibid., p. 112.

3. Ibid., p. 133.

4. Jean Gonick, "Perky, Polite, Perfectly Nice," *Self* magazine, (July 1989), p. 117.

5. Ibid.

6. Ibid.

7. Ibid., p. 118.

8. Ibid.

9. Ibid.

10. Ibid.

11. Ibid., p. 119.

12. Ibid.

13. Ibid.

14. Ibid.

15. Ibid.

References

Adderholdt-Elliot, Marian. *Perfectionism: What's Bad About Being Too Good.* Minneapolis: Free Spirit Publishing, Inc., 1987.

Alcorn, Randy and Nanci. *Women Under Stress.* Portland: Multnomah Press, 1986.

Backus, William and Marie Chapian. *Why Do I Do What I Don't Want to Do?* Minneapolis: Bethany House Publishers, 1984.

Brandt, Dr. Henry. *I Want Happiness Now.* Grand Rapids: Zondervan Publishing House, 1987.

Brody, Jane. "Become a 'Type B'." *Reader's Digest,* April 1981, pp. 87-89.

Carlson, Dwight L. *Overcoming Hurts and Anger.* Eugene: Harvest House Publishers, 1981.

Croghan, J. "The Psychology of Art." *American Artist Magazine,* June 1987, p. 14.

Dowling, Colette. *Perfect Women*. New York: Summit Books, 1988.

Gonick, Jean. "Perky, Polite, Perfectly Nice." *Self* magazine, July 1989.

Gundry, Patricia. *The Complete Woman*. Garden City: Doubleday & Co., Inc., 1981.

Halpern, Howard M. *Cutting Loose (An Adult Guide to Coming to Terms with Your Parents)*. New York: Bantam Books, 1977.

Lester, Andrew D. *Coping with Your Anger*. Philadelphia: The Westminster Press, 1983.

Littauer, Florence. *How to Get Along with Difficult People*. Eugene: Harvest House Publishers, 1984.

Maxwell, John C. *Your Attitude*. San Bernardino: Here's Life Publishers, Inc., 1984.

Miller, Keith. *Sin: Overcoming the Ultimate Deadly Addiction*. San Francisco: Harper & Row Publishers, 1987.

Murray, William J. *The Church Is Not For Perfect People*. Eugene: Harvest House Publishers, 1987.

Ridenour, Fritz. *How to Be a Christian Without Being Perfect*. Ventura: Regal Books, 1986.

Sandford, John and Paula. *The Transformation of the Inner Man*. Tulsa: Victory House, Inc., 1982.

Seamands, David A. *Healing Grace*. Wheaton: Victor Books, 1988.

Seamands, David A. *Healing of Memories*. Wheaton: Victor Books, 1988.

Seamands, David A. *Putting Away Childish Things*. Wheaton: Victor Books, 1986.

Slaughter, Carolyn. *A Perfect Woman*. New York: Ticknor & Fields, 1984.

Wagner, Maurice E. *Put It All Together*. Grand Rapids: Zondervan Publishing House, 1974.

Walters, Richard P. *Anger - Yours and Mine and What to Do About It*. Grand Rapids: Zondervan Publishing House, 1981.

Warfield, Benjamin B. *Studies in Perfectionism*. Phillipsburg: Presbyterian and Reformed Publishing Company, 1958.

Warren, Neil Clark. *Make Anger Your Ally.* Garden City: Doubleday & Company, Inc., 1983.

Weisinger, Hendrie and Norman Lobsenz. *Nobody's Perfect.* Los Angeles: Stratford Press (no date).